THE WEATHER

This book belongs to:

Blue Sky

It is rare for the sky to be free of clouds for the whole day. Clouds form when moist air cools. The sky looks blue because sunlight is scattered by our atmosphere. The cleaner the air, the bluer the sky is. If there was no atmosphere, what colour would the sky be?

I-Spy 5 for a blue sky Double with answer

Cirrus

This cloud is formed from ice crystals. It is often at a height of 6 to 8 kilometres. Cirrus clouds are frequently shaped into plumes and wisps by high-level winds and then they are known as mares' tails. If cirrus cloud thickens into a sheet, it can be the first sign of an approaching low-pressure system, and rain is likely. A typical 48-hour sequence of events when an area of low pressure crosses Britain is cirrus cloud, followed by cirrostratus, altostratus, and nimbostratus. When this clears, it is followed by cumulus and cumulonimbus with some showers.
I-Spy for 5

Cirrostratus

This sheet, or layer, of high-level cloud is made of ice crystals and is often the forerunner of rain. The sun may shine weakly through the cloud, and a ring or halo can often be seen around the sun or moon.

I-Spy for **5**

Cirrocumulus

This is a delicate, high-level ice cloud which is often in the form of ripples or dapples, or it may be fleece-like. Cirrocumulus clouds are often very beautiful but they are less common than cirrus. They indicate a deterioration in the weather.

I-Spy for **10**

Altocumulus

Altocumulus is a medium-level cloud found at heights of 4 to 6 kilometres. It consists of water and ice crystals. It can take various shapes which may be 'saucer-like', long rolls, regular patches and billows forming a 'mackerel sky', or even turret shapes. If these clouds increase and thicken, they are a sign of approaching bad weather.

I-Spy for **5**

Altostratus
Altostratus cloud forms a grey sheet at a height of about 4 kilometres. It can be thin enough to allow the sun to shine through it as though through frosted glass. Rain is only a few hours away.
I-Spy for **5**

Nimbostratus
The rain cloud is a dense layer at a height of about 2 kilometres. Rain or snow falls from it. Often there are patches of broken cloud below moving quickly in the wind. Nimbostratus forms as air is lifted over a wide area in a low-pressure system.
I-Spy for **5**

Stratus
This is a low, dull, grey layer of cloud which often shrouds the hilltops as it has here. Sometimes the wind breaks it up into scudding, fast-moving patches. Although this cloud produces only light drizzle, rain often falls through it from nimbostratus cloud above.
I-Spy for **5**

Fair-weather Cumulus

This cloud forms at a height of about 1 kilometre when bubbles of warmed air rise as thermals. The air then expands and cools so that the moisture condenses out to form the 'cotton-wool' clouds commonly seen on a summer's day. This process is called convection.

I-Spy for 5

Stratocumulus

When cumulus clouds merge, especially on a breezy day, they become more of a layer and this is called stratocumulus cloud. It is the most common type of cloud.

I-Spy for 5

5

Cumulonimbus

Cumulonimbus cloud can tower up to 10 kilometres or more and brings heavy showers or thunderstorms. Such clouds are formed when the atmosphere allows thermals to soar to great heights. If there is enough moisture in the air, large clouds develop. This happens especially in the summer.

I-Spy for **5**

Mamma

Mamma is sometimes seen on the underside of a cumulonimbus cloud. It looks like folds or 'pouches'. It is caused by descending cool air which falls earthwards from the top of the cloud.

I-Spy for **20**

Castellanus

These clouds are a type of altocumulus and look like the turrets of a castle. They often suggest that there will be thundery weather within a day or so.

I-Spy for 30

Billow Cloud

Billow cloud is seen at its best at about sunset. It can be a high- or medium-level cloud and is caused as winds aloft move at different speeds and often in different directions, too.

I-Spy for 10

Banner Cloud

Banner cloud may form on the lee side of a mountain peak. The wind eddies and lifts, and, if it is moist enough, cloud resembling a banner or flag will form.

I-Spy for 25
Double if you can recognize this famous Swiss mountain

'Wave' Cloud

More properly called lenticularis, this type of cloud is more common in hilly or mountainous regions where air currents are forced over a range. 'Wave' clouds have a smooth appearance. Sometimes, they are mistaken for flying saucers. This is another type of altocumulus.
I-Spy for **5**

Contrails

These are artificial clouds which form from the vapour trails of jet aircraft at a height of 9 kilometres. Water droplets freeze at these altitudes and, in effect, form cirrus clouds. If they last for a long time and form extensive layers, then it can be a sign of worsening weather.
I-Spy for **5**

Distrail

Sometimes aircraft cause clouds to evaporate because of the heat from their engines. This is called a distrail and is a long, clear patch in a cloud sheet.
I-Spy for **30**

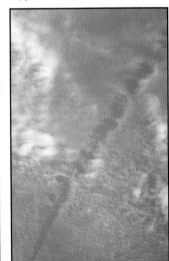

Artificial Cumulus

Artificial cumulus clouds may form over a power station when warm moist air rises and then cools.
I-Spy for **10**

Red Sky at Night

'Red sky at night, shepherds' delight' has some truth because most of our bad weather comes from the west. If the setting sun can be seen, there is no rain cloud for at least 300 kilometres upwind. The red colour is caused by dust and other particles in the atmosphere.
I-Spy for **5**

Yellow Sky to End the Day

'Yellow sky to end the day means wind and rain are on the way.' A yellow tint to the sky at sunset is often a sign of unsettled weather, particularly when this is accompanied by a turquoise, greeny blue sky overhead. Dust, salt particles, and increasing humidity in the atmosphere produce the colour.

I-Spy for **20**

Halo Round the Sun

'A halo round the sun or moon means that rain will be along quite soon.' It is formed as the light is refracted (bent) through ice crystals. Sometimes you can see colours: red on the inside with yellow and blue on the outside, although it is often white. Rain can be on the way if the cloud thickens soon after. **Never** look directly at the sun.

I-Spy for **20**

Corona

A corona is a series of rings around the sun or moon. Very often, though, it is just a blurred light with a brownish-red colour on the outside. It is caused by light from the sun or moon passing through water droplets in cloud much lower than that of a halo.

I-Spy for **20**

Mock Sun

A 'mock sun' or parhelion is an image of the sun refracted by ice crystals. There is often a reddish tint towards the real sun. In this picture the sun is to the left. A mock sun is often associated with haloes and approaching bad weather: 'Mock sun, dry on the run'. Twelve hours after this photograph was taken, it rained.

I-Spy for **10**

Mares' Tails

'Mares' tails, mares' tails, make tall ships carry low sails.' This is cirrus cloud that resembles plumes or tails. If it invades the sky and thickens, it is a sign of rain. The picture was taken at 7.30 am showing cirrus in the west and, by 7.30 pm, it was raining.

I-Spy for **5**

Mackerel Sky

'Mackerel sky, mackerel sky, never long wet, never long dry.' This cloud consists of small cells of either cirrocumulus or altocumulus. It resembles the scales of a fish. A mackerel sky indicates increasing moisture in the air aloft, and that can mean worsening weather.

I-Spy for 10

Mountains and Cliffs in the Sky

'When mountains and cliffs in the sky appear, some sun but violent showers are near.' When cumulus clouds begin to tower like this, it means that the atmosphere is moist and unstable. Thermals can reach great heights and form towering shower clouds. Summer thunderstorms often start in this way.

I-Spy for 5

Anvil Cloud

An 'anvil' cloud is a common sight in April. It is a cumulonimbus cloud where the top has spread sideways indicating drier, slowly sinking air about 5 kilometres above the ground. It looks like a blacksmith's anvil. This cloud gives the showers for which April is famous. 'March winds and April showers bring forth May flowers.'

I-Spy for 10

Rainbow

A rainbow occurs when sun shines on raindrops. The light is split into a spectrum of colours by refraction and reflection. Red is on the outside of the bow and violet on the inside. This is a primary rainbow. Sometimes, there may be an outer, secondary rainbow or even very faint inner bows called supernumeraries. A rainbow in the early morning means that there are showers upwind.

I-Spy for 10
Double for a double bow

13

Sun Pillar

A faint sun pillar is seen here. This is caused by the reflection of the setting sun shining on ice crystal cloud.

I-Spy for 30

Ice Bow

Sometimes, you might see a vividly coloured arc almost overhead. It can occur in cirrus cloud, and it is an ice bow. In this case, red is on the underside of the bow.

I-Spy for 30

Crepuscular Rays

Occasionally, especially just before or just after sunset, the sky shows lighter and darker area as the sun's rays are cut off by hills or mountains, and areas of cloud, dust, and other particles in the air are lit up. These crepuscular rays may be a beautiful pink colour.

I-Spy for **15**

Aurora

An aurora is caused by electrical discharges from the sun coming into contact with the outer parts of Earth's atmosphere. The atmosphere then glows at a height of 90 kilometres or more. This is most likely to happen when there is a lot of sunspot activity. An aurora looks like a curtain of coloured light in the sky. It is often seen in northern Scotland but only rarely in southern England.

I-Spy for **30**

Cones and Berries

Cones and berries are supposed to predict the weather. Some cones do close up when there is a lot of moisture in the air and open in dry weather to release their seeds. Keeping them indoors in a dry, centrally heated room is not useful. A crop of berries just shows that there has been a good spring, not that there is a harsh winter to come!

*I-Spy **5** for a good fir cone*
Was it open or shut?

Weather House

Human hair lengthens or shortens according to how dry or damp the air around us is. The weather house uses a human hair to forecast the weather. When the lady comes out, it is supposed to be fine weather while, when the gentleman emerges, the weather is poor. Hardly fair on the gentleman!
*I-Spy for **20***

Scarlet Pimpernel

The scarlet pimpernel is an annual plant that grows wild in Britain. It is sometimes known as the 'poor man's weather glass' because its orange-red petals close up when air becomes moist, so this is said to forecast rain. In this photograph taken in early afternoon, the flowers were closed. It rained within twenty-four hours! Check the petals at midday. What sort of weather followed?

*I-Spy for **10***

Rain

A day is 'wet' if more than 1 millimetre of rain falls. When more than 4 millimetres per hour falls, this is called heavy rain. The heaviest rainfall in twenty-fours hours in Britain was recorded at Martinstown, Dorset with 279 millimetres. The world record is 1870 mm. True or False?

I-Spy 5 for a rainy day — double with answer

Shower

Rain that falls from an individual cloud and lasts for less than fifteen minutes is called a shower. In this picture, 'virga' or streaks of falling rain can be seen as well as the clearance behind the shower.

I-Spy 5 for a shower
Double for virga

Snow

Snow is precipitation in the form of ice crystals. Crystals collect together into snowflakes. On average, snow lies on the ground for between ten and twenty days away from the coasts in Britain, but for more than sixty days in the Scottish Highlands. Snow is rarely more than 20 centimetres deep in low-lying places. Sleet is partly melted snow or snow mixed with rain. How many sides do the ice crystals have?

I-Spy for 10
Double with answer

Hail

Hail is made up of ice pellets in various shapes and sizes although most are rounded. In cumulonimbus clouds, violent upcurrents of air carry water droplets to heights where they freeze. Repeated rising and falling produces layers of ice and the pellets eventually plunge to the ground. Giant hailstones can be as big as large grapefruit. Hailstorms can destroy crops, damage buildings, and kill animals.

I-Spy for 10, or 50 if the hailstones are as big as a large grape

Lightning

A thunderstorm is associated with cumulonimbus clouds. A giant spark is created as ice crystals and water droplets within the cloud are split by air currents and collisions so that an electrical charge builds up. The spark creates temperatures of up to 30 000 °C. The rapid expansion of air causes a shock wave which produces the clap of thunder.
*I-Spy for **10***

Tornado

A tornado is a violently spinning mass of air made visible by a funnel-shaped cloud. In countries like the United States, it can bring wind speeds of 800 kilometres an hour. Fortunately, in Britain they are much less powerful but can still damage roofs and up-root trees. Tornadoes can occur when cold air rapidly takes the place of warm, moist air at a weather front or within violent thunderstorms. On a hot summer's day in Britain a small whirlwind may develop and pick up dust and straw. It is called a 'dust devil'.
*I-Spy **20** for a dust devil — double for a funnel cloud*

Gale

A wind is called a gale when its speed averages 34 knots [63 kilometres an hour (39 mph)] for a period of at least ten minutes. It can be measured by an anemometer or on the Beaufort Scale devised by Francis Beaufort in 1805. Here is a rough sea whipped up by a wind blowing steadily at 64 km/h (40 mph) . . .

I-Spy for **20**

Calm

. . . and a calm without a breath of wind. What forces are the gale and the calm on the Beaufort Scale?

Gale: _____

Calm: _____

I-Spy for **10**
Double scores with answers

Dew

Dew is formed especially in calm, clear conditions at night when air cools quickly and can no longer hold its water content as vapour. Little droplets condense on to blades of grass or spiders' webs, for example.

I-Spy for 5

Frost

Frost occurs when the temperature falls below 0 °C and ice crystals are deposited instead of dew. This is called hoar frost and can be very beautiful.

I-Spy for 5

Fog

Cloud close to ground level is called fog. It is made up of tiny water droplets. Fog reduces the distance you can see to less than 1000 metres. There are several types of fog. In this photograph, air has cooled overnight under clear skies. Cold, heavy air has condensed its moisture into small droplets. This is radiation fog. Look out for it just after dawn over meadows, lakes, and rivers.

I-Spy for 5

Haze
The distance we can see, the visibility, can be reduced by dust, sand, or salt particles as well as by fog. This photograph shows a hazy day during a heat wave. In a big city, in some weather conditions, fumes from cars may be trapped to form a haze which is a danger to health.
I-Spy for 5

Rime
Sometimes, even though the temperature is below freezing (0 °C), there are still water droplets in the air. These can freeze on contact with cold objects to form rime. Rime can be thick enough to resemble snow.
I-Spy for 15

Glaze

Occasionally, after a long cold spell, rain may fall on to frozen ground to form a 'glaze'. The rain freezes on contact with roads, pavements, trees, and telephone wires. It can be very dangerous for road users and pedestrians alike, and can even bring down power lines.
I-Spy for 40

Drought

Several weeks without rain is called a drought. In 1893, parts of London experienced seventy-three rainless days in a row during spring. When the weather is also hot, rivers and ponds dry up. In this picture, the National Rivers Authority had to rescue fish from a dried-up pond during the hot summer of 1990.
I-Spy 30 for signs of drought

Snow Drift
Snow can be fun when skiing, tobogganing, or making a snowman. But it can block roads and close railway lines, especially when strong winds cause powdery snow to drift. Look out for the fascinating shapes that snow drifts can form.
I-Spy for **10**

Snow Plough
Snow ploughs are used to clear roads or railways that have been blocked by snow.
I-Spy for **10**
Double for a rotary blower

Signs

Road signs may warn motorists that the road ahead is blocked by snow. Others may warn of ice on the road, or fog. You might see a sign warning of thin ice on a lake.

I-Spy 10 for each of four weather-related signs

Salt/Grit Bin

You will often see salt or grit bins on hills. Salt lowers the temperature at which water freezes and will help ice on the road to melt. Salt or grit on the road allows the traffic to get a better grip on icy or snow-covered roads.
I-Spy for 5

Flood

Flooding is another hazard that can affect motorists. It can also wash away a farmer's crops or ruin a person's home. Flooding can be caused by a sudden violent downpour or by prolonged rainfall.

I-Spy **10** *for a flood warning sign . . .*

. . . and **10** *for a flood*

River Level Gauge
Some places, such as along-side rivers or close to the sea, are especially liable to flooding. You might find a gauge like this one to measure river levels . . .
I-Spy for 10

Flood Marker
. . . or a marker to show the levels of past floods.
I-Spy for 20

Flood Prevention Scheme
This is the Thames Flood Barrier.
I-Spy 30 for any flood prevention scheme

Wind Damage

High winds can wreak havoc on land and at sea. In October 1987, more than fifteen million trees were blown down by winds reaching hurricane force across southern England.
I-Spy for 10

Wind Warning Sign

Some stretches of road are very exposed and, in windy weather, strong gusts are likely.
I-Spy for 10

Sunny Day on the Beach

In a summer heatwave, it is a good time to visit the beach. Often it is cooler here because of a breeze blowing in from the colder surface of the sea. What time of the day is the breeze strongest and why?
I-Spy for 10 — double with answer _____

Stevenson Screen

A weather station is an area set aside for measuring the weather. One of the most noticeable objects is a Stevenson Screen, designed by Thomas Stevenson, father of the author Robert Louis. It is a white, louvred box which allows air to pass through. It houses various instruments, particularly thermometers.

I-Spy for 15

Thermometers

Inside the Stevenson Screen there is a maximum thermometer which is set by shaking. It uses mercury and has a constriction at one end to prevent the mercury falling back as the temperature drops. A minimum thermometer uses alcohol that contains an index that moves as the liquid contracts. It is reset by tilting the tube.

I-Spy for 15

Wet Bulb Thermometer

You can recognize this thermometer by the muslin wick around the bulb. The wick leads into a reservoir of distilled water. It is used to measure how much water vapour is in the air. The greater the difference between the temperature it shows and that of an ordinary 'dry' bulb thermometer the less humid it is.

I-Spy for 20

Grass Thermometer

The temperature at ground level is important because this is where plants and crops begin to grow. A grass thermometer is put over the blades of grass and records minimum values. The temperature at this level is much colder on a clear night but warmer by day.

I-Spy for **15**

Soil Temperature

Soil temperature is very important to farmers and growers because plants will not grow if the temperature is too low. Temperature is measured at different depths. This is measured either using a bent-stem thermometer shaped in a right-angle, or within a metal tube sunk into the ground.

I-Spy for **15**

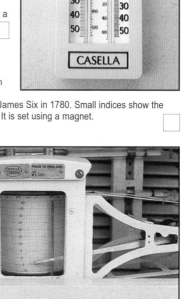

Hair Hygrometer

The hair hygrometer measures humidity. Hair expands when it becomes more humid and it turns a pointer. It works in a similar way to the weather house.
I-Spy for 10

Six's Thermometer

Thermometers may be used in greenhouses or on north-facing walls in gardens and conservatories. This U-shaped thermometer was invented by James Six in 1780. Small indices show the maximum and minimum temperatures. It is set using a magnet.
I-Spy for 10

Thermograph

It is useful to have a continuous record of temperature. A thermograph provides this by making a trace on a rotating drum. You might see one at coastal weather stations or ski resorts. They are also used in factories and in some offices where temperature has to be monitored.
I-Spy for 20

Rain Gauge
A rain gauge is a copper cylinder with a sharp-edged brass rim 125 millimetres in diameter and situated about 30 centimetres above soil level. The pattern shown here is called a Snowdon gauge.
I-Spy for **10**

Measuring Cylinder
Rain water is emptied from a rain gauge into the measuring cylinder which is graduated in millimetres.
I-Spy for **10**

Tilting Syphon Rain Gauge
People, like farmers and water engineers, need to know how much rain has fallen over a short period of time. A violent storm can give over 50 millimetres of rain in an hour causing flash floods and much damage to crops. In this gauge, the rain is directed into a vessel. A float with a pen records a trace on a graph. The steeper the trace, the heavier the rain.
I-Spy for **30**

The Four Winds

It can be said that Britain lies at the 'crossroads of the world's weather'. From the north-west, cool winds blow from Greenland and, often, there are showers. The north-east wind is 'neither good for man nor beast'; it brings us cold and sometimes snowy weather from Scandinavia and Russia. South-westerly winds from the Atlantic ocean blow mild, moist air towards us. And, in summer, south-easterly winds from southern Europe can lead to a heatwave and a rush to the beach.

Wind Sock

A wind sock, made of cloth or plastic, indicates wind strength and direction. The stronger the wind, the closer to horizontal the sock streams out from its pole. You will see them at airports but this one was being used by a school.
I-Spy for 10

Cup Anemometer

You will often see a cup anemometer with a vane at a weather station. It measures the strength and direction of the wind. Either the number of rotations is monitored as the wind blows or it is recorded electrically on a remote display unit.
I-Spy for 10

33

Hand-held Anemometer
This portable instrument is used by yachting enthusiasts, for example.
I-Spy for 10

Ventimeter
This is also used to measure wind strength. The wind blows through a small hole and raises either a small polystyrene ball or plate. A school may have a ventimeter.
I-Spy for 10

Wind Vane

A wind vane may crown a church spire or tall building. Wind vanes can be very decorative. The vane moves according to wind direction. Sometimes, a metal rod, called a lightning conductor, may be part of the vane or it may be separate.
I-Spy for 10
Double if it has a lightning conductor

Clues from Nature

If trees or bushes have been bent in one direction, it suggests that they have been shaped by the prevailing wind, that is, the most usual wind direction. You can often see this on hills or at the coast. In Britain, the most frequent wind direction is from the south-west.
I-Spy for 15

Aneroid Barometer

Barometers measure the weight of air pressing down at the surface, that is, atmospheric pressure. A good rule is that high pressure suggests that settled weather is likely while low pressure brings unsettled conditions. In an aneroid barometer air pressure pushes on a drum inside which is linked to levers that move the pointer.

I-Spy for 10

Mercury Barometer (below)

In this type of barometer, a column of mercury rises or falls according to changes of pressure. One kind is called a Fortin barometer. Who invented the mercury barometer and in which century?

I-Spy for 20 — double with answer

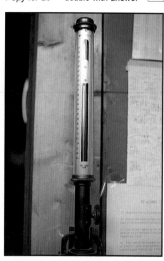

Barograph

In this instrument, the barometer is linked to an inked pen which draws a trace on paper on a rotating drum. These fascinating instruments often show the rapid pressure changes which are common in Britain. You may see them on display in shop windows or at seaside resorts.

I-Spy for 15

Fitzroy Barometer

This instrument is named after Admiral Robert Fitzroy. It includes rules for reading the pressure and for making a forecast. Admiral Fitzroy was the first person to issue forecasts for shipping in the 1850s.

I-Spy for 40

Weather Display

You will often see weather displays at popular tourist spots. Here temperature, pressure, and humidity are shown. Sometimes you may see an illuminated temperature display on a building.

I-Spy for 15

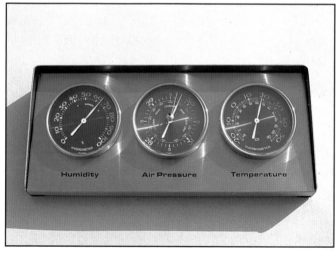

Sunshine Recorder

Often positioned on a high building, a Campbell-Stokes sunshine recorder is a glass sphere which focuses the sun's rays on to a card and scorches a trace or mark on it. This can be counted accurately in hours and minutes. In July 1911, Eastbourne and Hastings each measured 384 hours of sunshine. What part of the world has the most sunshine in a year, and where could you get the most sunshine in one day?

I-Spy for 30
Double with answers

Automatic Weather Station

Automatic weather stations are found more commonly now. This one is beside a main road near a junction with a motorway. Information from it can be used to report icy conditions, poor visibility, and high winds to traffic control centres.
I-Spy for 30

Weather Centre
There are fourteen weather centres around Britain. Weather information from around the world is gathered at the Headquarters of the Meteorological Office at Bracknell, Berkshire. Forecasts are produced with the help of 'super computers' and about 1100 scientists.
I-Spy for 25
Double for the Headquarters

Television Weather Forecaster
Almost everyone recognizes a television weather Forecaster. It is a skilled job to explain, in a few minutes, the often complicated weather patterns in Britain and Europe. This picture was taken in the stormy January 1990.

I-Spy for 5 — double if you know the name of the man in this picture

THE WEATHER FORECAST

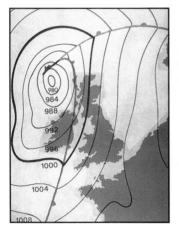

Weather Map

A weather map shows lines of equal pressure, called isobars, and also where low- and high-pressure systems are. It also has 'fronts', areas where different types of air collide and produce cloud to give rain or snow. Weather people often mention warm or cold fronts. They are indicated by lines with triangular or semi-circular marks.
I-Spy for 10

Weather Radar Tower

Radar can show where rain, snow, or hail is falling. The radar bounces a signal off the rain and its location and intensity are shown on a screen. Most weather radar towers now have an open lattice structure supporting the dome.
I-Spy for 50

Satellite Picture

Studying the weather from satellite pictures has helped weather forecasters greatly. They can look down from 40 000 kilometres to see half the world's weather at a glance. They can spot weather systems forming long before they reach our islands. There are five stationary satellites around the Equator while others orbit the Poles.

I-Spy for 10
Double for the name of any satellite

Television Radar Pictures

Radar pictures are often screened on television to show areas of rain or snow or even individual showers. Heavy and light rain are shown in different colours. Water engineers can use these pictures to locate rainstorms that might lead to flooding.

I-Spy for 15

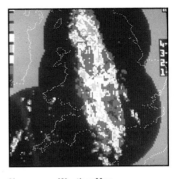

Newspaper Weather Map

Some daily newspapers print a weather map and forecast. This one comes from the Meteorological Office. Weather information also tells you what the weather was like around the world the day before. Which place was the hottest and which the coldest in the information you saw?

Hottest: _____

Coldest: _____

I-Spy for 5 — double with answers

Weather News

Newspapers and magazines often have accounts of weather events such as storms, floods, or freezes. Sometimes, they may look back at the weather over the month or year. Why not cut out the reports and keep them in a scrap book?

I-Spy for 10

Solar Panels
Britain is not one of the sunniest countries in the world. In London, however, there is still four hours sunshine a day on average, and the figure is higher on the south coast. Some people have fitted solar panels to the roofs of their houses to make use of the sun's energy.

I-Spy for 10

Sundial
In some gardens, or on walls as here, you may see a sundial to tell the time. At midday, the sun is due south and casts the shortest shadow. At what time of the year does the sun cast the shortest shadow at midday?

I-Spy for 10
Double with answer

Wind Generator
For centuries, windmills have made use of the wind's energy to drive machinery. Nowadays, many have fallen into disrepair but you may see wind pumps or wind-generating machines. Where would you expect the best places to be to locate wind generators in Britain?

I-Spy for 10
Double for a working windmill

Winter Sports

Snow can be a nuisance but it can be fun, too, and, in places like Scotland or the Alps, it is an important tourist industry.

I-Spy for **15**

On the Wind

Some craft, such as a sailing boat, a hot-air balloon, or a glider, depend entirely on which way the wind is blowing or the way thermals rise.

I-Spy **10** *for any of these*
Double if you can say which
direction the craft was travelling

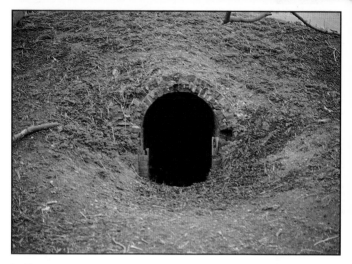

Ice House

Before the days of refrigerators, mounds were built in the gardens of large country estates in which ice or snow was stored. Iced drinks or puddings could be kept there in the summer, and vegetables stayed fresher, too.
*I-Spy for **40***

Reservoir

The rain that falls can be stored in artificial lakes to be used for irrigating crops, drinking water, or generating electricity, for example. This reservoir is very low

because of a prolonged drought. It should be full to the brim in February when this picture was taken. Rain and snow fall as part of the water cycle.

*I-Spy for **10***
Double if you can explain the water cycle

Spring Flowers

The growth of plants and their flowering times are affected by the weather. Studying when plants come into leaf or flower is part of the science called phenology (short for phenomenology). These spring plants are the first to flower.

I-Spy for **10**
Double for noting the date, or when trees come into leaf, or migrating birds arrive

What's in a Name?

Some places offered shelter from the weather. They were in high places or exposed areas, and the weather features in the modern place name. Similar places are Caldecote and Snowhill.
I-Spy for **20**

Look out, too, for pub and inn signs with a weather theme. This pub was built on the site of an 1836 avalanche.
I-Spy for **20**

Weather Roundabout
There is even a
roundabout dedicated to
the weather!
I-Spy for 50

Stamps
If you collect stamps, you
may find examples which
depict weather topics
such as on these
Swedish examples.
Countries, such as Qatar
and the Maldives, have
some excellent
examples.
I-Spy for 20